CONTENTS

DON'T FEAR HOW GREAT YOU CAN BE.

MERRITT MATHIAS AGE 29
PROFESSIONAL SOCCER PLAYER

PLAY LIKE A GIRL

Life Lessons from the Soccer Field

KATE T. PARKER

WORKMAN PUBLISHING • NEW YORK

This book is dedicated to all the women with whom I've had the honor and privilege of stepping on the field since I first played this game. It's been a gift to have you as teammates and friends.

Library of Congress Cataloging-in-Publication Data is available.

ISBN 978-1-5235-1136-5

Design by Rae Ann Spitzenberger and Lisa Hollander

Workman books are available at special discounts when purchased in bulk for premiums and sales promotions as well as for fund-raising or educational use. Special editions or book excerpts can also be created to specification. For details, contact the Special Sales Director at the address below, or send an email to specialmarkets@workman.com.

Workman Publishing Co., Inc.
225 Varick Street
New York, NY 10014-4381
workman.com

WORKMAN is a registered trademark of Workman Publishing Co., Inc.

Printed in the United States of America
First printing April 2020

10 9 8 7 6 5 4 3 2 1

INTRODUCTION

I can't remember a time when I didn't want to play soccer. As a very little girl, sitting on the sidelines of my older brothers' games, I had one thought running through my head the entire 90 minutes: *I want in. Whatever this game is . . . I want to play it.* I wanted to be running and pushing and kicking and sweating and scoring. I wanted to be on that field. I had never seen any girls play, but that didn't bother me. When I was seven, I begged my mom to find me a team, and she did—and the moment I put on my uniform, laced up my cleats, and stepped onto the field for the first time, I was hooked.

Seven-year-old me was pretty impatient (so is 43-year-old me. Some things never change!). I was also loud, pushy, and aggressive, with a quick temper. That combination of personality traits didn't make things easy for me on a day-to-day basis, but on the soccer field, things were different. Those characteristics that earned me labels like "difficult" or "bossy" off the field actually helped to make me a good—no, a *great*—athlete on the field. All the parts of me that other people tried to get me to soften or change, my coaches loved. My loudness and pushiness helped me win balls and score goals . . . and sometimes get yellow cards, but that's another story.

Me with my first team, the Rovers

I am now a mother of two fierce soccer-playing girls (both of whom you'll see celebrated in these pages), and I've coached countless others. But growing up playing soccer in the eighties, things looked very different. Female-only soccer teams were few and far between. We didn't see little girls wearing Megan Rapinoe and Alex Morgan jerseys to nationally televised games. Indeed, when I first started playing, I wanted to be just like my older brothers. It wasn't until high school that I came upon Michelle Akers in one of my soccer magazines, and then I wanted to be just like Michelle Akers, who was so good and so tough and so strong. Today, as a photographer dedicated to giving girls lots of good and tough and strong role models, I get to photograph Michelle Akers (page 139)! And not just Akers, but Jessica McDonald (page 128) and Carli Lloyd (page 156) and more than a dozen other players who are following in the footsteps of Mia Hamm, Brandi Chastain, and Abby Wambach, who showed us just how amazing women playing soccer could be.

Me, senior year of high school (Go Lions!)

And not just professional players, but athletes like my friends and former teammates Beth Foley (page 79) and Amanda Riepe (pages 154–155) who helped pave the way for the next generation by being members of the first collegiate women's soccer team that their school fielded.

These days, it is estimated that 30 million women are playing the game worldwide. Look no further than the popularity of internationally revered players like Christine Sinclair (Canada), Ada Hegerberg (Norway) or Marta (Brazil) to see the global phenomenon that women's soccer has become. Listen to these women, and then to yourselves, because now it is your time.

And that's what this book is about. Speaking personally, I can say that while I gave a lot to soccer (all that bottled up energy!), it gave more back to me. The field and locker room (and bus, and training room, and long runs) were the classrooms where I learned the most in my life about teamwork, sportsmanship, and determination—and they are all rules I continue to live by: *Keep Your Head Up. Play to Your Strengths. Find Common Ground. Make Every Minute Count.* I've learned that what your body can do is more important than what it looks like, that your teammates always will have your back and you should have theirs, sustenance is key, and that it's important to recognize and celebrate what you're good at and not be afraid to show it off a little bit. As you turn the pages and see and hear from the many soccer-playing girls and women I've had the good fortune to meet, you'll find those very versatile lessons—and more. Because no matter your age and no matter your experience, there are some universal truths when it comes to this beautiful game.

After photographing and meeting the amazing subjects in this book, I feel hopeful. Hopeful that our passions, like soccer, encourage us to be true to ourselves and live in pursuit of our dreams. By finding our voices on the field, we find it off as well. It inspired me to remember my superpowers, and that although I don't play soccer as much as I did when I was younger, those qualities that made me stand out on the field, make me stand out as a mom, as an author, as a business owner, as an advocate and photographer. This book helped me find my voice again and made me remember how much joy there is to be found within those white lines of the field.

There are so many voices telling us not to be who we really are. Sometimes it is hard to remember or figure out who that is. We don't have to listen to the "no"s or the "shouldn't"s. You can own your strength. You can celebrate it. You can play like a girl.

SOCCER HAS TAUGHT ME HOW TO BE A BETTER COMMUNICATOR.

AMISA AGE 13

KEEP YOUR HEAD UP

Anyone who has ever spent time on a soccer field knows this game can be tricky. One minute, you're winning and on top of the world, and the next, you're down 2–1 and your head is spinning. You don't quite know what happened or why. Maybe it was a pass that didn't quite connect, or an otherwise amazing shot that hit the crossbar. Soccer is fluid, and the game is always changing—just as in life. There are literally thousands of split-second decisions you make in a single game: Some end well, others not so much. Your job, as a player, is to stay connected, keep your head on a swivel, and anticipate what is coming next. Sometimes a player gets "unlucky," and when that happens, the very best thing she can do is keep going: No pouting, no moping, no complaining to the referee—because she'll miss the next play. You can't control your luck, but you can control how hard you work.

Unlucky doesn't mean you've failed. Unlucky doesn't mean you're done. It simply means you did the best you could, but in that split second, the goal, pass, win, just didn't happen. It also means that if you keep your head in the game, the next split second will go your way.

If you don't want
to be pushed, then
don't play soccer.

KARLEY AGE 14

Fight hard until the last whistle, and you can always hold your head high.

FIONA AGE 11

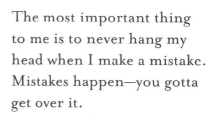

The most important thing to me is to never hang my head when I make a mistake. Mistakes happen—you gotta get over it.

ELLA AGE 14

I am learning to use only my feet.

PENELOPE AGE 3

Team sports instilled in me the confidence
to support and root for other women.
Cheering for your teammates on the soccer
field is a skill you can take into the workplace
and boardroom—because one woman's
success is a win for all women everywhere.

DEVNEY AGE 40

The biggest challenge that I have faced in soccer is wanting to be the best player I can be in a short period of time—when I started, all of my teammates had already been playing soccer for about five years.

ZAHARA AGE 12

YOU HAVE TO GROW AND BE PATIENT WITH YOURSELF. WHEN YOU MAKE A MISTAKE, IT'S ON TO THE NEXT PLAY.

ABBY SMITH AGE 26
PROFESSIONAL SOCCER PLAYER

Working as a team makes everything so much easier and so much more fun.

REGHAN AGE 14

I want to score goals and I want to pass the ball to my teammates. My dad teaches me new soccer moves. I love soccer and I believe in myself.

WINNIE AGE 6

As a holding midfielder, I need to know what's going on all around me, all the time. It's hard, and I have to be calm on the field, but I enjoy being in the center of the action.

SIYONA AGE 13

Soccer makes me think a few steps ahead. I like that about the game.

EJ AGE 9

Stepping on the field wearing pink in our hair means more than just a color. It is a tribute to my mom and the thousands of women who courageously fight breast cancer every day.

OLIVIA AGE 14

I am the smallest player on my team. And usually the field. And I don't let that bother me.

NATALIE AGE 11

FIND SOMETHING YOU'RE GOOD AT AND JUST WORK ON IT. IF IT'S BEING QUICK, IF IT'S BEING STRONG, IF IT'S YOUR LEFT FOOT, JUST WORK ON IT BECAUSE THAT'S WHAT CAN SET YOU APART.

ERIKA TYMRAK AGE 28
PROFESSIONAL SOCCER PLAYER

PLAY TO YOUR STRENGTHS

Look around at your teammates—sure, you can all run the length of the field ten times over, but aside from the basics, you're also all incredibly different. One girl is a tough-as-nails defender, one can dribble circles around her opponents, another is an aerial specialist, one has a rocket shot, and still another is the loudest voice on the field. The thing that will help you the most in life, as it will on the field, is to identify what sets you apart and use it most effectively to your advantage. There are 11 different positions on a soccer field, which means 11 different voices, skill sets, and personalities that all must work together as a single machine.

Diversity of skills is an asset on any team, so while your instinct may be to focus on improving your deficiencies, leaning into that skill that already sets you apart may be more valuable. Your team needs you—they need exactly what you bring to the field, what makes you special, and what makes you . . . *you*. And whether you are loud, aggressive, measured, scrappy, meticulous, crafty . . . the world needs that, too.

I have learned to play more
aggressively on the field,
like I do with my brother
and daddy at home when
we are practicing.

MEREDETH AGE 7

I was diagnosed with juvenile arthritis when I was 4. But soccer is also a part of me, so I keep moving and give it my all even when my JA tries to hold me back. I know my body might not be kind to me the next day, but it helps to know I can control the ball even if I can't control when my JA will flare up.

EMME AGE 8

The thing I love about soccer is that the size of your body doesn't matter. It's the size of your heart that does.

DANIELA AGE 11

Never let anyone turn
your sky into a ceiling.

CARSON PICKETT AGE 26
PROFESSIONAL SOCCER PLAYER

Soccer isn't about winning,
it's about how much fun
you have playing.

REESE AGE 10

I want to be the better sportsman both on and off the field.

CHLOE AGE 10

Focus on yourself and not on others.

ABBY AGE 11

Be aggressive. Just pretend that the ball is the last piece of food in the world and you have to fight for it.

ELOISE AGE 7

Being on a team forces you to learn to deal with all different types of people.

GABRIELLA AGE 11

During the milliseconds that your brain has to react to a save, it also has to tell you that what seems impossible is possible. And that is the hardest thing to do in soccer.

LISA AGE 17

FOCUS ON EFFORT RATHER THAN PERFORMANCE BECAUSE HARD WORK REALLY SHOWS.

KYLIE AGE 22

I was born in Sudan and raised in Kenya. Soccer means the world to me. It's the only thing that helps me clear my mind completely when I need it the most, and the game has made it easier for me to adapt to a new country, because I can connect with people on the field.

MAZZA AGE 13

I like kicking with both feet.

KAMDEN AGE 6

I play hard for the trophies.

SUTTON AGE 4

Kick like a girl. Throw like a girl.
Run like a girl. Be a cheetah!

SOPHIA AGE 7

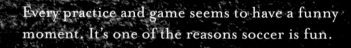

Every practice and game seems to have a funny
moment. It's one of the reasons soccer is fun.

HANNAH AGE 9

Great players come
in all shapes and sizes.

GIOVANNA AGE 11

When I was 5, I picked up
a ladybug during a game to
make sure it didn't get hurt.

EMAAN AGE 11

THE BEST THING AFTER A GAME IS LOOKING DOWN AT MY LEGS AND COUNTING ALL THE SCRAPES AND GRASS STAINS THAT WENT INTO IT.

RILEY AGE 14

CELEBRATE YOUR BODY

Your body is incredible, and you've earned it. Soccer, like most physical activities, isn't easy. The game asks a lot of its players: running, jumping, kicking, falling down, getting up, sliding, heading, falling again—and that's just practice. Did you know that the average distance run by a single player per game can be as great as 7 miles?

Sports are demanding of our minds, but most obviously of our bodies. You can often identify a soccer player's legs by their bruises, scars, sock or shin guard tan lines, and probably a raspberry or two. But the thing that stands out the most are their muscles. While the game has always been easy for me to love, I used to despise my soccer legs. Clothes never fit quite right, and I wished my legs were smaller. But I came to understand that if they didn't look the way they did, they wouldn't do all the things I asked of them. You need strong calves and quads to run hard for 90 minutes, the same way you need that callus on your writing hand to help you hold the pencil just right when you're drawing. You've helped shape your body in a way that makes it capable of skills and feats that others dream of. Bodies like yours can climb mountains, swim across lakes, and run marathons.

When I score a goal, I hear the parents cheering and clapping. It makes me feel like a hero. Then I look back and my teammates are smiling.

JESSIE AGE 11

Soccer taught me how to be tough and when to be nice, how to be more direct and when to be more of a leader.

JORDAN AGE 17

When I came out of the game, my friends started to cheer so loud for me and it made me feel amazing.

ELLA HART AGE 12

Same team. Same ACL injury. Same surgeon. Same surgery date. It's nice to have not only a teammate but a friend to recover with and to always remind you that the most important part of falling down is getting back up.

BELLA AGE 13

There is no better feeling than having the confidence in yourself to leave your heart on the field. I do everything I can to defend our goal.

JOJO AGE 14

If you love the game, you will work harder
than ever and enjoy every moment of the
game. It's when we stop loving the sport
that it feels like work.

MIAH AGE 25

I've learned in my life to never give up and I can do all things.

AVERY AGE 10

My teammates work together to bring out the best in each other.

LARA AGE 14

Nothing will ever
hold me back!

ANDREA AGE 11

Soccer is a lot more fun when
you laugh. I love to make my
teammates crack up.

POPPY AGE 7

We are proud of our muscles, bruises, and scars.
Our legs have a lot of stories to tell.

TELLER AGE 14

AS A DEFENDER, I'M INVOLVED IN A LOT OF TACKLES. I NEED MY MUSCLES. I CAN'T BE SUPER SKINNY. THAT'S NOT MY STYLE OF PLAY.

AMBER BROOKS AGE 29
PROFESSIONAL SOCCER PLAYER

I worked really hard. I went to the gym every day, practiced my footwork, and worked my body as hard as I could, and I still didn't make the team I wanted to. Sometimes that happens.

BRAYDEN AGE 12

It is beyond fun to be able to still meet up with great friends every Sunday to laugh, sweat, and exercise away life's stresses for a few hours.

JILL AGE 39

Everyone has different ways of seeing things, and you can always learn something new.

SERETH AGE 10

ON EVERY TEAM I'VE EVER BEEN ON, I REMEMBER THE PEOPLE MORE THAN ANYTHING ELSE.

HALEY KOPMEYER AGE 29
PROFESSIONAL SOCCER PLAYER

THE TEAM IS THE THING

As athletes, we know the bond we share as a team. What we may not know (or be able to comprehend) at 10 or even 20 years old is that this bond never ends. When you stop playing soccer because of injury or the sheer busyness of life (*if* you stop playing soccer—see CJ on page 162), you tend not to leave these friendships behind. Because once you've had their backs on the field, they'll have yours in life. Scientists have studied the ways in which human connections may be strengthened and deepened by shared intense experiences, and a sports team, especially as you get to higher levels of play, is a clear example of this—the relationship is a powerful one: You sweat together, you cry together, you lose together, you win together.

You are part of something much larger, and the soccer team experience allows you to honor your contribution to that whole and recognize how valuable every contribution is, whether your role is cheering from the bench, scoring winning goals in the waning seconds, shagging balls, or taking free kicks. You'll have been through it all together, and no matter what, your teammates will show up for you.

Don't be afraid of making mistakes or what your teammates will think. Focus on yourself and how you can get better. No one else can make you practice or get better—you have to put the time into it.

ALISON AGE 19

Traveling with my teammates is the best because we always run around together and do silly things. We make so many memories and become closer friends!

GABBY AGE 14

My life changed when I joined the US Deaf Women's National Team at age 15. I've been lucky enough to attend many international events, win a few gold medals, and meet some amazing people over the last decade. But the thing that changed my life the most has been being around people who are just like me.

KATE WARD AGE 26
PROFESSIONAL SOCCER PLAYER

SIGNING "USA SOCCER"
FROM L TO R:
SYDNEY NELSON, AGE 24
BETH BARBIERS, AGE 40
JULIA KELLEY, AGE 26
KATE WARD, AGE 25

Just being in this team environment, surrounded by such a great group of women, I'm able to leave all my emotions on the field and focus on soccer.

JESSICA McDONALD AGE 31
PROFESSIONAL SOCCER PLAYER

We win when we work together and are there for each other. I love my soccer girlfriends.

GABI AGE 11

Being vocal is part of
my job on the field.

HADLEY AGE 14

My teammates are my ride-or-die friends. I don't know what I'd do without them.

MIA AGE 9

It's okay to fail. It is never okay to give up.

NAKIA AGE 10

I love that I can let my inner bull out on the field and there are no hard feelings. Soccer peeps are definitely good sports.

BLAKELY AGE 11

I feel like my legs are going to fall off. Ice baths are supposed to help, but four minutes is a long time!

RACHEL AGE 14

We've been friends since preseason in 1994. That's a lot of laughs, tears, games, weddings, babies, husbands, parties—but mostly laughs. Being teammates is more than just being friends. We're sisters.

BETH AGE 43

I LOVE PLAYING SOCCER WITH MY FRIENDS. WE LAUGH A LOT AND MAKE IT FUN.

CAROLINE AGE 8

Soccer has taught me that
it's important to overcome
your fears and it's okay to be
tough when you are a girl.

ALINE AGE 10

When you make new friends
in soccer, you will always have
friends outside of soccer.

ALEXA AGE 10

CONTROL THE CONTROLLABLES.
AS LONG AS YOU HAVE DONE
ALL YOU CAN DO AND GIVEN
ALL YOU HAVE, YOU
CAN BE HAPPY
ABOUT YOUR
CONTRIBUTION.

KRISTEN EDMONDS AGE 32
PROFESSIONAL SOCCER PLAYER

MAKE EVERY MINUTE COUNT

In a soccer game, there are only 90 minutes (less time if you're younger) to prove yourselves as a team. It means there's zero time to mess around. Whistle to whistle, you need to hustle. Keep your eye on the clock, pace yourself, and trust that there will be time for rest and rehydration (half time! weekends!). Know your limits, but when you show up, respect the time that everyone has taken to do the same.

In life, the scale of time is broader, but the work ethic is the same. If you imagine your daily experiences like a soccer game, there will be goals to celebrate and perfect moments when you feel completely in sync with those around you, and then other times when it all seems unfair and you feel alone. Those are the times when it's extra important to persevere, minute by minute, in order to keep improving. Because, as goalkeeper Haley Kopmeyer says, "No matter the situation, you can outwork talent by digging in and giving it as much as you possibly can." On and off the field: Work hard. Work smart. Work together.

I didn't actually get
this bruise from soccer.
I walked into a wall.

CLAIRE AGE 11

My favorite part
of practice is when
we get to mess
around and laugh.

SYDNEY AGE 7

GOOOAAAALLLLL!!!

ALICE AGE 8

I played in a soccer game the afternoon after my sister's funeral. That's what Grace would have wanted me to do. Playing in that game helped me to forget and remember all at the same time. For me, soccer is more than a sport, it's a grounding force. It helps me keep my feet on the ground when things are falling apart and all that is important in life seems to be floating away.

CAROLINE AGE 14

I adore soccer and I am so thankful to still be playing. I was invited to go play in a tournament in Hawaii and I am going!

BETSY AGE 62

I'm from Congo but I was raised in Uganda. Back home, we didn't have a lot of female soccer teams because people thought soccer was a sport that only men can play.

ESTHER AGE 13

Be the change you want
to see—in your team,
in your school, in life.
Call people up rather
than calling them out.

MADISON AGE 14

TOO OFTEN PEOPLE FOCUS ONLY ON THE SUCCESS—RAISING THE TROPHY, OR THE PROMOTION—THEY DON'T KNOW THE STRUGGLE IT TOOK.

MERRITT MATHIAS AGE 29
PROFESSIONAL SOCCER PLAYER

My mom tells me all the time, "Own your mistakes and move on." Blaming the refs, your team, or the field is not good. It's something I work on now with everything: If it was my fault, I own up to it and learn from it.

PRESLEY AGE 9

I have a ritual when I throw the ball in: I start exactly seven steps back, which is my lucky number. As I approach the line, I toss the ball in my hands. We use my throw-ins as set pieces to score. It's not just a throw-in—it's one that's going to the goal.

AVERY AGE 16

My team is a tribe of girls that always has my back.

SOPHIA AGE 13

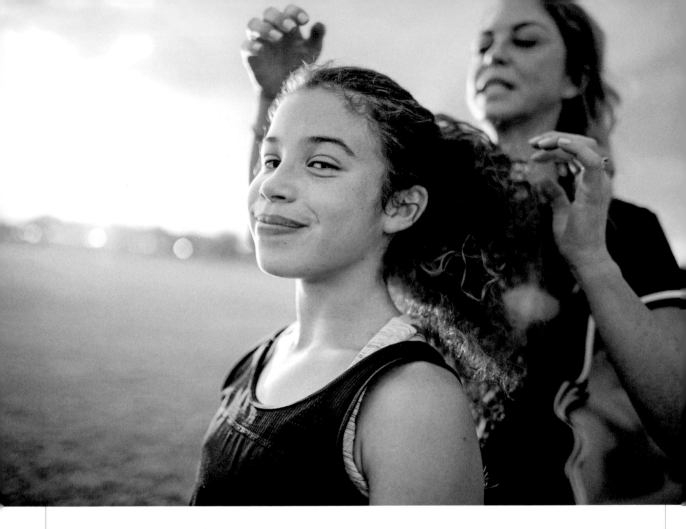

I hope to be a strong role model for my daughter so that one day she can be an even stronger role model to others, just like my mom was to so many girls and women.

DANA AGE 42

You call it a foul,
I call it fun.

HARRIET AGE 12

The thing about soccer is
that the more you practice,
the better you get. I guess
most things are like that.

ELLA AGE 14

When I hit the
field, I feel like
I can do anything.

CHARLOTTE AGE 11

Sitting is something
I cannot do.

DYLAN AGE 11

THIS IS MY CHARGE TO EVERYONE: WE HAVE TO BE BETTER. WE'VE GOT TO LOVE MORE, HATE LESS. WE'VE GOT TO LISTEN MORE, TALK LESS.

MEGAN RAPINOE AGE 34
PROFESSIONAL SOCCER PLAYER

FIND COMMON GROUND

Every time your team steps on the field, you're walking on common ground shared with 11 other athletes who eat, sleep, and breathe soccer just like you do. Or when you think more broadly, it's ground shared with 265 million players around the world. Soccer, or football, as most other countries around the globe refer to it, is the world's most popular sport—it's also one of the most accessible. At its most basic, you don't need much more than a ball to kick around in order to play.

Soccer has the effect of making the world feel smaller, and when you have something so universal in common, it's easy to recognize that we are all more alike than we are different. As a player, you may have the opportunity to travel internationally or play teams from another country or state. As a fan, you can catch high-level professional, college, or international play on screen almost any time of day. The styles are all so different: Some countries' play feels almost lyrical, some teams play with strict precision, some are cautious, some are crafty. But no matter how complicated the strategies can be, the game is fundamentally simple the world over: Get the ball into the back of the net.

I've been cut. I've been benched. I've been injured. They were all hard in their own way, and each took a different amount of time for me to overcome. Like my eyeliner? It's not. It's a black eye from an elbow.

CARI ROCCARO AGE 25
PROFESSIONAL SOCCER PLAYER

My heroes are mostly soccer players.

ALICE AGE 11

I haven't scored a goal yet, but I've only been playing for a year. It will come.

KENSLEY AGE 8

Playing on a team is like nothing else you'll ever do in life. You share the highest highs and lowest lows. It's emotional, exhilarating, and complex—and there's nothing else like it.

BECCA MOROS AGE 34
PROFESSIONAL SOCCER PLAYER

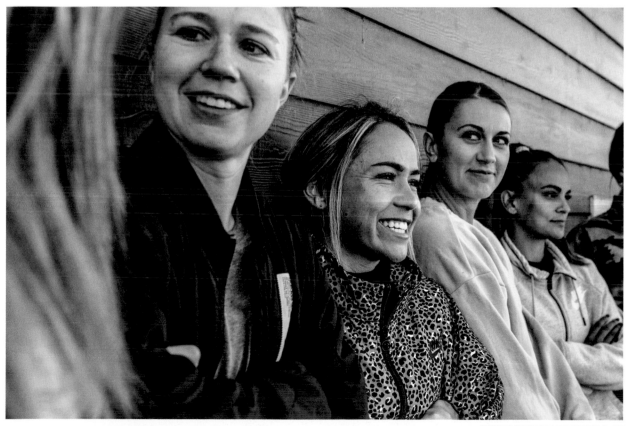

I stand for love. In honor of the game that first taught me love, that I still love, and that helps me love my teammates as they are—unique, special, love-worthy people—I want to encourage a culture where everyone is free to express themselves on the field and off.

KATIE STENGEL AGE 27
PROFESSIONAL SOCCER PLAYER

Never take yourself too seriously or be too hard on yourself when you mess up. Stay positive.

KATE AGE 12

I didn't even know I hurt
myself until I came off the
field. Bloody noses happen
in soccer. I'm okay.

CARSON AGE 11

As a young girl in Jerusalem, I had no opportunity to play football (soccer). The exclusion of women from football is only a part of their marginalization in society, which is a state of things we aspire to change. I helped create the first space for women and girls to play the game. Through football we combat stereotypes, help shatter glass ceilings, and encourage women to step into a better reality.

DAPHNA AGE 34

It's my birthday. I brought cupcakes to practice.

ALEXA AGE 8

My teammates are the kind
of people I want to surround
myself with in life.

LEAH AGE 12

I plan to play for a
long time, through
college at least.
When is that again?

PHIFER AGE 7

With the right coach and attitude,
I think I can do anything.

KRISHA AGE 7

My mother always said that soccer was a man's sport. At school, I heard the same thing. Growing up in Brazil, I could only play when the boys' team needed a player, so I was always hoping someone was out so I could have a chance!

KIKA AGE 34

Anytime I need to stand up, raise my voice, and fight for what I need—especially when it comes to my job in a very male-dominated sphere—I have soccer to thank.

JÚLIA AGE 30

Part of my pregame
and practice ritual is
organizing my hair.
I can make a ponytail
or braid with my eyes
closed and with no
bumps.

AVERY AGE 16

Soccer is my anger management.

RILEY AGE 12

We're hydrating.

TAYLA AGE 7

It's always important to have my game face on.

ABBY AGE 9

I'VE BEEN ABLE TO PLAY WITH MY SON BY MY SIDE, AND HAVING HIM WITNESS EVERYTHING HAPPENING IN MY CAREER IS TREMENDOUS. HE'S GOING TO REMEMBER THIS. AND HE IS WHAT I'M WORKING HARD FOR.

JESSICA McDONALD AGE 31
PROFESSIONAL SOCCER PLAYER

DON'T USE YOUR HANDS

Use your head and your heart instead. Sure, there's the actual rule against soccer players using their hands (unless you're a goalkeeper or executing a throw-in, hands are meant for high fives!), but the real game-changer for a player is what she brings to the field beyond her physical talent. Anyone can improve her technical style of play, but it's those moments when it's all heart and guts that real strength is revealed.

Out on the field, it can be easy to stay hidden. You can run around all day, without making any impact on the game. But that's playing it safe. Sure, any time you enter into a play, you risk losing the ball or making a mistake, but it's also how you learn— *and* how you win. Demand the ball when you're open. Make runs. Get open if you're not. Speak up. Be confident. Be smart. Use the skills and talents— and grit—that you have. Because with risk comes reward.

Do all of this *on* the field—and then go do it *off* the field. Don't be afraid of what might happen if you speak up or make waves or ask for what you deserve.

When I walk off
the field with my
knees scraped and
my face sweaty,
I know I played
with all my heart.

ALEX AGE 10

I first played soccer when I was in fifth grade. I was still new to America and I wanted to try something new, so I joined my school soccer team and started to learn slowly with the team. When I play, I feel relief and calm.

MIRACLE AGE 13

I like playing soccer
like my mama.

SUTTON AGE 4

No matter the outcome, my mom is always there for me.

KELSIE AGE 14

Soccer has been invaluable in all aspects of my adult life. It really trained me in how to be a human being.

ERIN AGE 39

Sometimes getting along can be hard, but at the end of the day you are a team, and team is family.

KATHERINE AGE 11

My mommy
screamed really
loud when I
made a goal.

EMMA AGE 5

We all share the same
love of the game.

MAGGIE AGE 9

At the professional level, almost everyone has the physical tools to be the best. It comes down to a few things: how bad you want it, what you do when things get hard, and whether you are able to stay focused amid turmoil, challenge, chaos, and demands. It's all in your head and in your heart.

MICHELLE AKERS AGE 53
PROFESSIONAL SOCCER PLAYER

One time at camp, a girl was being made fun of for being short. I told the older girls to stop being mean. I stood next to that girl, and she knew she had me by her side to stand up for her, so she didn't have to stand alone. My mom tells me I can be brave, strong, and powerful—and I can.

ADA AGE 7

Soccer has shown me the way: how to be tough, but with a sense of humor.

CAROL AGE 38

I HAD BACK-TO-BACK ACL TEARS IN DIFFERENT KNEES IN 8½ MONTHS. OVERCOMING THAT AND GETTING BACK TO PLAYING WAS THE HARDEST THING I'VE EVER DONE, BUT SO WORTH IT.

JOANNA FENNEMA AGE 24
PROFESSIONAL SOCCER PLAYER

I love to play. The adult coed leagues can be tough sometimes. Men often still assume that female players are less valuable, so it's been hard feeling like I have to prove that I'm just as capable, if not more, than they are.

KAYLA AGE 27

This was my first
practice in the rain.
I will remember this
night forever.

CALISTA AGE 8

I get nervous before my games. I'm jittery in warm-ups and my heart races. But once the whistle blows and I make my first run or pass, the nerves just go away. Every time.

ALICE AGE 11

I BROKE MY ARM AND THAT SAME NIGHT HAD PRACTICE FOR MY CLUB TEAM. I DIDN'T WANT TO MISS IT. I WON'T LET A BROKEN ARM STOP ME. MY DAD WRAPS MY CAST IN FOAM EVERY GAME.

CAILEY AGE 11

THE BETTER TEAM DOESN'T ALWAYS WIN

Sometimes you win, sometimes you lose. The outcome of the game can be determined by factors out of your control. It's not always the more athletic or talented team that wins. There are times when you may fail despite all signs pointing to yes. We've all been there: exhausted, defeated, frustrated, confused. The effort just wasn't reflected in the score.

When you get to this point, the very best thing you can do is to simply let it go. Exhale. Then inhale and try to recognize that you can't control everything, on the field or off. If the things within your control (like how hard you work and your attitude) showed up to play, then pat yourself on the back and move on. If not, then focus on the controllable aspects that you can improve upon.

Team wins and losses are important, but in the face of a devastating loss, remember the smaller victories as well. Did you finally hit 100 juggles? Did you master a new move? Are you making progress coming back from an injury? Approaching these goals with a good work ethic determines the kind of player (and person) you are.

As the parent of an athlete, what makes
me most proud is her fighting attitude
and leaving it all on the field. Sometimes
you win and sometimes you don't, but
giving it your all is what matters most.

JESSICA AGE 42

I love playing soccer, but most of all I love my team.

LUCY AGE 10

I take being captain
very seriously.

ELLA AGE 9

The only person on your journey with you the whole time is you. Your parents are there for you, your friends are there for you, but it's you who has to really believe in yourself in order to succeed.

MANDY LADDISH AGE 27
PROFESSIONAL SOCCER PLAYER

I played soccer my entire life. I'm grateful to be able to give back to these girls and teach them about this game that has given me so much.

AMANDA AGE 43

LIFE IS GOING TO THROW ALL KINDS OF OBSTACLES IN YOUR WAY. ALL I CAN TELL YOU IS WHAT WORKS FOR ME: BE TRUE TO YOURSELF, DON'T DO FAKE, AND ABOVE ALL ELSE, KEEP ON WORKING BECAUSE THAT'S WHAT WILL TAKE YOU WHERE YOU WANT TO GO. **CARLI LLOYD** AGE 37 PROFESSIONAL SOCCER PLAYER

It's just an arm. I can still dribble, pass, and shoot just fine.

DANIELA AGE 11

I learned how to be
confident on the field.
Now, I am more
confident at school.

MEREDETH AGE 7

Teammates wipe off your tears,
Throw away your fears;
Help you when you fall,
Making you feel twice as tall.
They are your best friends
And maybe even your family.
So when you fall down
They always come back around.

MEGAN AGE 11

Excuses sound best to
the person making them
up. Strength and growth
come from tackling the
changes ahead of you.

KALEIGH KURTZ AGE 25
PROFESSIONAL SOCCER PLAYER

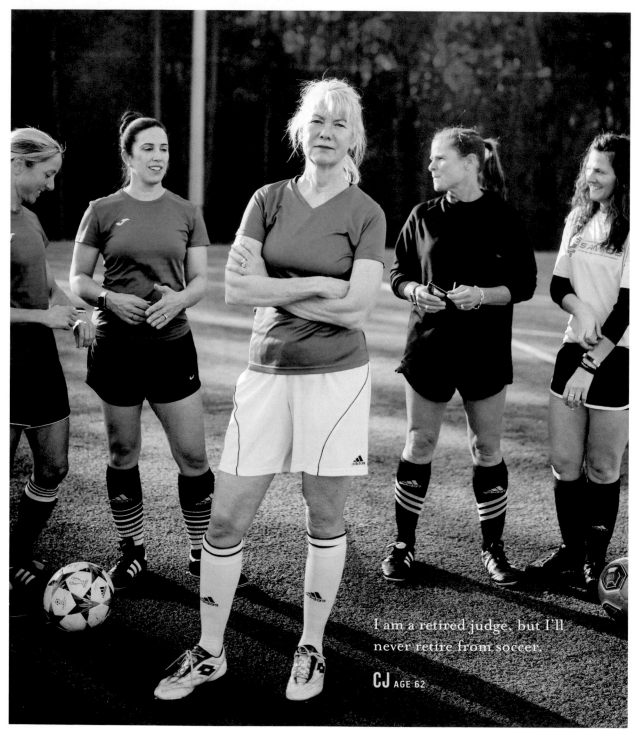

I am a retired judge, but I'll never retire from soccer.

CJ AGE 62

Injuries are no fun, but my teammates make it a lot better.

AVA AGE 10

My first year as a pro, I was cut from the team midway through the season. I didn't know if I should leave the game or give it another go. I stayed to train with the team for the remainder of the season and took every coaching job I could find. In the offseason, I hired a coach and got a job just to pay him. I made the team the next season. I'm so proud I made the decision to invest in myself.

HALEY KOPMEYER AGE 29
PROFESSIONAL SOCCER PLAYER

After six concussions, I had to stop competing. It's not what I had planned. But soccer memories and life lessons are still part of who I am, and soccer will always be my passion even though I am no longer wearing #11.

EMMA AGE 16

Regionals. July in Louisiana.
I am the only keeper, and I
was up all night throwing up.
I still went out and played
because it is what I love to do.
(We won.)

ELLA AGE 14

ALWAYS PACK SNACKS

Soccer is a workout. And it can be punishing. Whether it's just running around on the grass at practice or higher-level ball work, stretching, weights, and agility, you demand a lot from your body mentally and physically. If you don't take care of yourself, the sport, like life, can leave you exhausted and depleted. Athletes need sustenance, and not just the water jugs and orange slices served up on the sidelines—though those help, too (as do the bandages and ice packs)! But apart from eating and hydrating and healing, it's important that you're able to figure out what fills you back up when your body and mind want to quit. Is it curling up on the couch at home, hanging with friends, laughing with family, making art or music, or reading a book while you ice that new injury?

Some players, like professional player McCall Zerboni (who credits soccer with keeping her out of trouble), look to the sport as an escape from life—a "place where I'm not thinking about things—where I feel free and released." But what happens when you need an escape from soccer? The seasons are long, and the physical and mental toll that soccer can take on your body has a way of accumulating. Identify what your orange slice is, and you'll be in good shape.

Whether you win or lose,
there's always something
to celebrate.

BELLA AGE 11

There's nothing better than feeling that your team is like family.

JORDAN AGE 10

I told you I could do it.

KALI AGE 5

State champs!

LULU AGE 14

Whether I miss or score, my
teammates always lift me up.

GIANNA AGE 9

This sport can be a huge time commitment, and you may miss out on a lot of things, but it will all be worth it. The relationships you build and the work ethic that you create will last a lifetime.

MACKENZIE AGE 17

My teammates and I are weird. We know it,
and we like being different.

MEG AGE 12

Sometimes you have to remind yourself that soccer isn't the most important thing in life. My support system, my friends, and my family mean the most to me. They are what really fulfill me.

LILY AGE 22

AS KIDS, WE HAD THIS DREAM OF SOMETHING WE COULD BE OR SOMEONE WE COULD BECOME. NOW KIDS CAN ACTUALLY LOOK AND SEE WOMEN AS ROLE MODELS AND SOCCER PLAYERS, AND I THINK IT'S GOING TO HAVE SUCH AN IMPACT.

McCALL ZERBONI AGE 33
PROFESSIONAL SOCCER PLAYER

You can't score if you
don't take a shot.

BIANCA AGE 11

You always need to take the
time to rest, to hydrate,
and get your energy back.

SADI AGE 12

There's nothing better
than being myself.

KENDAL AGE 11

Our moms used to
play together, and
now they coach us.

MIA AGE 8

SOMETIMES I DON'T WANT TO PLAY. THERE'S OTHER STUFF I WANT TO DO. BUT I KNOW THAT IN THE LONG RUN, THE CHOICE TO WORK HARD IS ALWAYS A GOOD ONE.

ELLA AGE 13

KEEP UP THE FIGHT

There are enough challenges on the field that it's hard to imagine taking your voice or platform to a stage wider or broader than the lines on the grass. But soccer-as-metaphor-for-life is especially applicable when you see how players across all levels of the game take the confidence that they develop on the field and apply it to their struggles off the field.

Professional female soccer players have been fighting for equal pay since the first women's league was formed. Many young athletes, like Ada (page 140), know how to stand up against bullies. The ability to fight for what you want or believe in is remarkable and should not be wasted. You know how to fight to win a ball or a tackle or an entire game, but you also know how to fight for equal pay or to start the first girls' team in your town. There are so many inequities and challenges that you are equipped to help change or meet. You are immensely stronger and more powerful than you think—getting more so every day. Stay with it. Keep improving the game for yourself. Keep improving the game for others.

I am a goalkeeper, so my
fingers are all in some state
of being broken or sprained.
It comes with the job.

LISA AGE 17

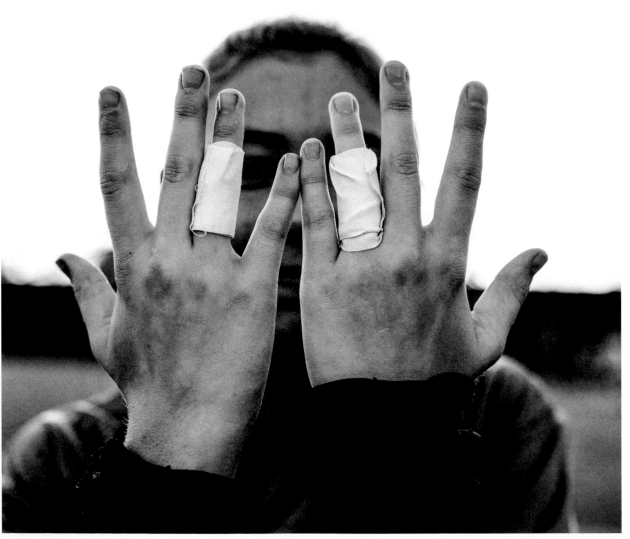

Squad goals.

ALICE AGE 11

We like our water breaks.
They're good for water
but also messing around.

SARAH AGE 8

There's a time and a place to be selfish. Soccer has taught me that. In certain situations you have to be selfish and you will be rewarded, but in other situations you can't be. It's a very fine line.

TAYLOR LYTLE AGE 30
PROFESSIONAL SOCCER PLAYER

I tore my left ACL three times in five
years, but I think I became a stronger
player and person through the process,
and I would never want that to be taken
away from me. I want us all to feel
pride in showing our scars.

JORDAN ANGELI AGE 33
PROFESSIONAL SOCCER PLAYER

Once I missed an open goal and my teammate told me I was bad at soccer. It hurt my feelings and I lost my confidence, but I kept playing and did my best.

SOPHIA AGE 8

The worst feeling in the world is when you want to play, but can't. Being on the sidelines is no fun, but it makes me really appreciate when I am out there.

ALICE AGE 11

BE STUBBORN IN THE MOST POSITIVE WAY POSSIBLE. ANY TIME YOU FACE A NEW OBSTACLE, REFUSE TO ACCEPT IT. FIGHT IT.

LO'EAU LaBONTA AGE 26
PROFESSIONAL SOCCER PLAYER

When I was in high school, I wanted to play for my school, but there was no girls' team, so I joined the boys' team—it was the only choice. My team always stood up for me despite the ridicule I got from opposing teams. I love that now I can still play this game with my sister.

JANICE AGE 57

Forget about the
glass slippers, these
princesses wear cleats.

IVY AGE 11

When people tell you no,
just smile and tell them
"Yes, I can."

JULIE FOUDY AGE 48
PROFESSIONAL SOCCER PLAYER

It's okay to be assertive and strong and fight for your position on the field. It works off the field, too, when you learn to stand up for yourself.

JORDAN AGE 14

APPENDIX:
ABOUT THE WOMEN IN THIS BOOK

DEVNEY PREUSS *(page 11)* held her first job as a soccer and basketball youth league referee. As an adult, she worked for the Phoenix Suns (men's basketball) and on the Super Bowl Host Committee, and is now a president and CEO who plays competitive soccer.

ABBY SMITH *(page 15)* started her career as a goalkeeper for the Boston Breakers, and has since gone on to play for the Utah Royals and the Western Sydney Wanderers in the Australian W-League.

ERIKA TYMRAK *(page 26)* was a midfielder for FC Kansas City and then Utah Royals, as well as Bayard Munich in Germany, until her retirement in 2020.

CARSON PICKETT *(page 30)* has played as a defender for teams including Seattle Reign FC, Orlando Pride, and Brisbane Roar in Australia's W-League.

KYLIE MINIEFIELD *(page 35)* is a former midfielder and captain of the Arizona State University women's team.

MIAH HIPP *(page 52)* is the coach for an Under-11 Girls' YMCA team that offers children of all ages and abilities opportunities to enjoy soccer.

AMBER BROOKS *(pages 60-61)* is a defender who has played for the Portland Thorns, Seattle Reign, and the Houston Dash. Brooks holds the NWSL record for consecutive minutes played for three years running.

JILL REYES *(page 64)* has been playing soccer for more than 30 years. Her experience playing as a goalkeeper taught her skills that she uses every day.

HALEY KOPMEYER *(pages 66, 164)* started her professional career as goalkeeper for Seattle Reign FC and has since gone on to play for the Orlando Pride.

SYDNEY NELSON *(page 70)* played on the US Deaf Women's National Team from 2011-2012. She was on the winning US national team at the Deaf World Cup in 2012.

BETH BARBIERS *(page 70)* has played with the US Deaf Women's National Team and many other soccer clubs. She also represented Team USA as a member of the Track and Field team at the 2017 Deaflympics.

JULIA KELLEY *(page 71)* played Division I soccer at Kennesaw State University as an outside forward/midfielder. She was a member of the US Deaf Women's National Team from 2011-2013, and won the Deaf World Cup in 2012 and the Deaflympics in 2013. She shares the Golden Boot for both tournaments.

KATE WARD *(page 71)* joined the US Deaf Women's National Team in 2009 as a midfielder. She is also assistant coach at the University of Texas at El Paso. She played on the US team that won the Deaf World Cup in 2016.

JESSICA McDONALD *(pages 72, 128)* began her career with the Chicago Red Stars before going on to play for a number of other teams, including Seattle Reign FC, Houston Dash, North Carolina Courage, and more—and the USWNT. She is a FIFA Women's World Cup Champion (and the only mom on the roster in 2019) and was the first NWSL player to reach 33 regular-season goals.

BETH FOLEY *(page 79)* played defense for Wake Forest University's first women's varsity soccer team. She is now an interior designer who uses the skills she learned on the field to defend her clients' interests.

KRISTEN EDMONDS *(page 84)* is a midfielder who began her pro career in 2011 on the Stjarnan Women's team in Iceland. She has since played in the NWSL for WFC with the Orlando Pride.

BETSY ABRAMS *(page 91)* is a midfielder who has loved the game for as long as she can remember. She soloed in an airplane when she was 16, worked as a meteorologist for

22 years, has traveled to all seven continents, and is the captain of her recreational soccer team.

MERRITT MATHIAS *(pages 94-95)*, a defender, has played with FC Kansas City, Seattle Reign FC, and North Carolina Courage. She also played for the winning USWNT at the 2018 Tournament of Nations.

DANA HOOPER *(page 100)* is a sports attorney and agent who balances life with her daughters and husband with playing competitive adult soccer. She played collegiate soccer, went on to attend law school, and now blends her passion for sports with her legal career as a law school professor, teaching Professional Sports Law, and an agent representing a variety of athletes and sports-related clients throughout the world.

MEGAN RAPINOE *(page 106)* has played for over a decade on the national level on teams including the Philadelphia Independence and MagicJack of the WPS, the Chicago Red Stars and Reign FC in the NWSL, Sydney FC in Australia's W-League, and Olympique Lyonnais in France. As a member of the USWNT, she is an Olympic gold medalist, two-time FIFA Women's World Cup Champion, and The Best FIFA Women's Player winner of 2019. She won the Golden Boot Award for most goals during the 2019 FIFA World Cup and the Ballon d'Or Feminin 2019 awarded to the best player in the world.

CARI ROCCARO *(page 109)* began her professional career as a defender for the Houston Dash in 2016 and has since played for the North Carolina Courage.

BECCA MOROS *(page 111)* has played at the professional level for the Washington Freedom, MagicJack, and Western New York Flash in WPS and for FC Kansas City, Houston Dash, Utah Royals FC in the NWSL as well, as INAC Kobe Leoness in Japan.

KATIE STENGEL *(page 112)* has played as a forward at the professional level for the Boston Breakers, Washington Spirit, Utah Royals FC, and the Houston Dash.

DAPHNA GOLDSCHMIDT *(page 115)* is the first woman in Israel to serve as chairperson of a professional sports club, the Hapoel Katamon Jerusalem Football Club. She works to create programs that foster gender equality in sports.

KIKA BRANCO *(page 121)* is a Brazilian sports journalist who has reported for TV Galo and Club Atlético Mineiro. Branco works to support women's sports, which often struggle due to lack of funding and societal prejudices.

JÚLIA VERGUEIRO *(page 122)* is the owner and CEO of Pelado Real Futebol Clube, a soccer group in Brazil that runs girls' soccer clinics and training sessions for adult women.

ERIN REGAN *(page 134)* is a former goalkeeper for the Washington Freedom during the 2003 season. She has since become a firefighter. She and other female firefighters cocreated Girls Fire Camp, a program that gives teenage girls a chance to shadow real firefighters.

MICHELLE AKERS *(page 139)* is a decorated midfielder and forward who played on the USWNT from 1985-2000. She is a two-time FIFA Women's World Cup champion and won the Golden Boot Award during the 1991 FIFA World Cup. She is an Olympic gold medalist, the FIFA Female Player of the Century, and a National Soccer Hall of Fame inductee.

CAROL BARCELLOS *(page 141)* is a nationally renowned Brazilian sports journalist and the founder of the Destemidas ("Fearless") project, which provides athletic training to young women in Rio de Janeiro's underserved communities and works to inspire women across Brazil to break gender barriers through sports.

JOANNA FENNEMA *(page 143)* played as a midfielder for UNC Chapel Hill before joining the Chicago Red Stars and then the Orlando Pride in the NWSL.

KAYLA SOBBA *(page 144)* works at Georgia Soccer, the authorized State Youth and Adult Soccer Association made up of over 100 local affiliates and leagues that works to promote, grow, and develop soccer.

JESSICA MILLER *(page 150)* is a soccer mom who fell in love with the sport through watching her daughters fall in love with it. She is an Ivy League graduate, retired consultant, and cancer survivor, but her most important title today is Team Manager for her daughters' team.

MANDY LADDISH *(page 153)* spent her professional soccer career as a midfielder with FC Kansas City and the Utah Royals FC before retiring in 2020.

CARLI LLOYD *(pages 156-157)*, a forward and midfielder, has played for over a decade on the professional level on teams like the Western New York Flash, Houston Dash, Sky Blue FC, and the USWNT. Lloyd is a two-time Olympic gold medalist and two-time FIFA Women's World Cup champion. She was named FIFA Player of the Year in 2015 and 2016, and became the first player ever to score three goals in a FIFA Women's World Cup final in 2015.

KALEIGH KURTZ *(page 161)* started her career with Östersun DFF, a Swedish team in the Elitettan league. She has since played as a defender for the North Carolina Courage in the NWSL as well as Canberra United in Australia's W-League.

CJ MELLO *(page 162)* is a retired judge and current soccer player who has played for Georgia United (co-ed), Emerald Express, and any pickup game she can get to. She has played in Japan, Portugal, Denmark, and all over the United States.

AMANDA RIEPE *(pages 154-155)* is a former collegiate soccer player. She has dedicated her career to the health care and real estate fields, and spends her free time coaching.

LILY SCHNEIDER *(page 177)* Lily is a former midfielder and defender for the Wake Forest women's soccer team, where she majored in communications and minored in economics.

McCALL ZERBONI *(pages 178-179)* is a veteran midfielder who has played on the Western New York Flash, Portland Thorns FC, Boston Breakers, North Carolina Courage, and Sky Blue FC.

TAYLOR LYTLE *(page 189)* is a midfielder who has played on professional teams including Sky Blue FC and the Utah Royals FC.

JORDAN ANGELI *(page 190)* played professional soccer for the Boston Breakers, Washington Spirit, and the Western New York Flash. She has since worked as a host, analyst, and play-by-play commentator for various professional broadcasts including the FIFA World Cup. She is also the founder of the ACL Club.

LO'EAU LaBONTA *(pages 194-195)* has played professionally as a midfielder for Sky Blue FC, FC Kansas City, and the Utah Royals FC, as well as for the Western Sydney Wanderers in Australia's W-League.

JANICE GIVENS *(page 196)* has played one season of soccer almost every year since 1970. She worked for the Men's World Cup in 1994, the Women's World Cup in 1999, and the soccer venues at the Atlanta Olympic Games in 1996. A two-time breast cancer survivor, she says that the desire to get back on the field sped up her recovery.

JULIE FOUDY *(page 198)* is a retired midfielder, two-time FIFA Women's World Cup champion, and two-time Olympic gold medalist. She played for the USWNT from 1987-2004 and was the team's captain from 2000-2004. She was the first American and first woman to receive the FIFA Fair Play Award in 1997, served as president of the Women's Sports Foundation from 2000-2002, and was inducted into the National Soccer Hall of Fame in 2007.

ACKNOWLEDGMENTS

This book, just like the game it is about, was a team effort. I would not have been able to create this without the help, guidance, and advice of some amazing people.

I am so thankful, first and foremost, to the girls and women who grace these pages. Thank you for loving this game. Your words and images are so powerful, and you are making a difference in sharing them. Thank you for trusting me.

As always, I couldn't do this without my family. Mike, Ella, and Alice (and Tobin and Mabel), I love you beyond measure. We are truly a soccer family, and I can't think of a more perfect weekend than watching you girls take the field (and maybe getting in a game myself). A huge thank-you to my very large and supportive family. Mom and Fran, thank you for finding a team for a soccer-obsessed seven-year-old. Thank you for driving me to state practices in Manalapan on a weekday. Thank you for never really caring how I played, but more about who I was. Dave and Steve, you were my role models, and you always pushed me to try harder and do better. I believed in myself because you did. Meg, I just realized you've probably attended hundreds and hundreds of games with zero interest in the sport . . . you're a saint. I love you.

Dana Hooper, you are a rock star. When I go pro, you're definitely my first choice as agent. Seriously, thank you for your belief in this project. You were an invaluable part in making sure that strong, confident, and capable women like yourself were represented among these pages.

Sari Rose, you are a veritable Rolodex of soccer folks. The breadth and diversity in this book is in huge part thanks to you. Thank you. Roswell Santos Soccer Club, thank you for teaching my kids to love this game and for being so generous with your players and facilities. Thank you to my alma mater, Wake Forest University, and Tony and Courtney, for allowing me to share the stories of their women's team. Much appreciation goes to Soccer in the Streets for introducing me to their inspiring program. Thank you to Atlanta Academy for your incredible support over the years and for always lending me your beautiful campus for shoots.

Mike, thank you for keeping this book organized and on track, two things you very well know that I could never do without you. William Callahan, I always know you have my back and fully trust your insight. Thank you for believing in this and my work from the beginning. Jen Brabant, you're so good at what you do, advocate fiercely and always make us laugh. Thank you to you, Mitch and Taylor. Lou #3, thanks for being my sounding board for the last 26 years. Wouldn't want to do any of this without you. Rogers and Cowan, thank you for believing in this message so strongly and getting the word out there.

And finally, thank you to everyone at Workman for believing in my work and this project. Megan Nicolay, our fourth book together! It's been a privilege to work with someone as smart and thoughtful, and who cares as much as you do. Thank you. Rae Ann Spitzenberger, thank you for making this book beautiful. Chloe Puton, Beth Levy, Julie Primavera, Barbara Peragine, Sarah Curley, Katie Campbell, and the entire team—thank you. It's a joy to create books that matter with you.

YOU JUST HAVE TO KEEP SHOWING UP.

BECCA MOROS AGE 34
PROFESSIONAL SOCCER PLAYER